EXTRA INNINGS

Baseball Poems

SELECTED BY LEE BENNETT HOPKINS

ILLUSTRATED BY SCOTT MEDLOCK

HARCOURT BRACE JOVANOVICH, PUBLISHERS

SAN DIEGO   NEW YORK   LONDON

Requests for permission to make copies of any part of the work should be mailed to:
Permissions Department, Harcourt Brace Jovanovich, Publishers, 8th Floor,
Orlando, Florida 32887.

Permission acknowledgments appear on page 40, which constitutes a
continuation of the copyright page.

Library of Congress Cataloging-in-Publication Data
Extra innings: baseball poems/selected by Lee Bennett Hopkins;
illustrated by Scott Medlock.
p.   cm.
Summary: A collection of nineteen poems about baseball, including
playing and watching the game.
ISBN 0-15-226833-2
1. Baseball—Juvenile poetry.   2. Children's poetry, American.
[1. Baseball—Poetry.   2. American poetry—Collections.]
I. Hopkins, Lee Bennett.   II. Medlock, Scott, ill.
PS595.B33E97   1993
811.008'036—dc20   92-13013

First edition
A B C D E
PRINTED IN SINGAPORE

The paintings in this book were done in oil on paper.
The text type was set in Weiss
by Thompson Type, San Diego, California.
Color separations by Bright Arts, Ltd., Singapore
Printed and bound by Tien Wah Press, Singapore
Production supervision by Warren Wallerstein and Fran Wager
Designed by Lisa Peters

For my father, Leon Hall Hopkins (1915–1989),
with thanks for the few extra innings.

—L. B. H.

For my dear wife, Myrna, and my parents, Nancy and Frank,
with appreciation for their lifelong encouragement and support.

—S. M.

Contents

Analysis of Baseball

May Swenson

It's about
the ball,
the bat,
and the mitt.
Ball hits
bat, or it
hits mitt.
Bat doesn't
hit ball, bat
meets it
Ball bounces
off bat, flies
air, or thuds
ground (dud)
or it
fits mitt.

Bat waits
for ball
to mate.
Ball hates
to take bat's
bait. Ball
flirts, bat's
late, don't
keep the date.
Ball goes in
(thwack) to mitt,
and goes out
(thwack) back
to mitt.

Ball fits
mitt, but
not all
the time.
Sometimes
ball gets hit
(pow) when bat
meets it,
and sails
to a place
where mitt
has to quit
in disgrace.
That's about
the bases
loaded,
about 40,000
fans exploded.

It's about
the ball,
the bat,
the mitt,
the bases
and the fans.
It's done
on a diamond,
and for fun.
It's about
home, and it's
about run.

1

Playing Outfield

Isabel Joshlin Glaser

The baseball drops into your glove,
Sounds like . . . *Thunk!* (or *Plunk?*
Or *Plop? Whop?*) . . . but stays,
Sounds like . . . another sunny day,
Dust, sweat shivering down,
Clothes plastered to your skin,

    THIRST . . . .

Sounds like you caught a flier,
The other side's out,
And your team leads,
Everybody's yelling like crazy,

    HOORAY!

                water, please . . .

Let's Go, Mets
[Opening of the 1984 Season]

Lillian Morrison

Mookie and Hubie and Strawberry,
These are the guys in the lineup for me.
Hernandez can hit, play first base with style,
Foster comes through every once in a while.
But for hustle and muscle and artistry,
Give me Mookie and Hubie and Strawberry.
These are my hopefuls, these are my three:
Mookie and Hubie and Strawberry.

from At Little League

Patricia Hubbell

Nine little boys, loose-jointed, run,
Connect, slide home, make outs;
Two cry.
      The worried adults dart their eyes.
      All are too intent but one.
      Mr. Dunne, the phys ed teacher from the school,
      Watches with a cool elan,
      Noting how his boys progress,
      Involved, yet uninvolved, and keen.
      Twenty fathers, middle-aged,
      Fight off fatigue,
      Heft bats, toss balls,
      And dream, inside their after-office brains,
      Of how, with any luck at all,
      They would have scored the winning run,
      Have pitched the perfect game.

To a Baseball

Anonymous

You're going into play? An instant more
      And yours the eyes of thousands. There's
            for you
Huge plaudits welcoming the needed score,
      Deep disapprovals at misplays they view,
And, best of all, the eager silence there
When, swift from bat or hand, you hang in air.

To Satch
[or American Gothic]

Samuel Allen

Sometimes I feel like I will *never* stop
Just go on forever
Till one fine mornin'
I'm gonna reach up and grab me a handfulla stars
Swing out my long lean leg
And whip three hot strikes burnin' down the heavens
And look over at God and say,
How about that!

Prediction: School P.E.

Isabel Joshlin Glaser

Someday
when the baseball's
          hurtling
like some UFO,
          blazing
like some mad thing
          toward me
                    in outfield
I *won't* gasp
and dodge. Oh, no!
Instead, I'll be
calmer than calm
          — so la-de-da! —
I'll just reach out
          like a *pro*
and catch it and — quick! —
          throw to second.
And everyone will say, "Hooray!
Natalie made a double-play!"
Some day.

Casey at the Bat

Ernest Lawrence Thayer

The outlook wasn't brilliant for the Mudville nine that day;
The score stood four to two with but one inning more to play.
And then, when Cooney died at first, and Barrows did the same,
A sickly silence fell upon the patrons of the game.

A straggling few got up to go in deep despair. The rest
Clung to that hope which springs eternal in the human breast;
They thought, If only Casey could but get a whack at that
We'd put up even money now, with Casey at the bat.

But Flynn preceded Casey, as did also Jimmy Blake,
And the former was a lulu and the latter was a cake;
So upon that stricken multitude grim melancholy sat,
For there seemed but little chance of Casey's getting to the bat.

But Flynn let drive a single, to the wonderment of all,
And Blake, the much despised, tore the cover off the ball;
And when the dust had lifted, and men saw what had occurred,
There was Jimmy safe at second, and Flynn a-hugging third.

Then from five thousand throats and more there rose a lusty yell;
It rumbled through the valley, it rattled in the dell;
It knocked upon the mountain and recoiled upon the flat,
For Casey, mighty Casey, was advancing to the bat.

There was ease in Casey's manner as he stepped into his place;
There was pride in Casey's bearing and a smile on Casey's face.
And when, responding to the cheers, he lightly doffed his hat,
No stranger in the crowd could doubt 'twas Casey at the bat.

Ten thousand eyes were on him as he rubbed his hands with dirt,
Five thousand tongues applauded when he wiped them on his shirt;
Then while the writhing pitcher ground the ball into his hip,
Defiance gleamed from Casey's eye, a sneer curled Casey's lip.

And now the leather-covered sphere came hurtling through the air,
And Casey stood a-watching it in haughty grandeur there.
Close by the sturdy batsman the ball unheeded sped;
"That ain't my style," said Casey. "Strike one," the umpire said.

From the benches, black with people, there went up a muffled roar,
Like the beating of the storm waves on a stern and distant shore.
"Kill him! Kill the umpire!" shouted someone on the stand.
And it's likely they'd have killed him had not Casey raised his hand.

With a smile of Christian charity great Casey's visage shone;
He stilled the rising tumult, he bade the game go on;
He signaled to the pitcher, and once more the spheroid flew;
But Casey still ignored it, and the umpire said, "Strike two."

"Fraud!" cried the maddened thousands, and echo answered "Fraud!"
But one scornful look from Casey and the audience was awed;
They saw his face grown stern and cold, they saw his muscles strain,
And they knew that Casey wouldn't let that ball go by again.

The sneer is gone from Casey's lip, his teeth are clenched in hate,
He pounds with cruel violence his bat upon the plate;
And now the pitcher holds the ball, and now he lets it go,
And now the air is shattered by the force of Casey's blow.

Oh, somewhere in the favored land the sun is shining bright,
The band is playing somewhere, and somewhere hearts are light;
And somewhere men are laughing, and somewhere children shout,
But there is no joy in Mudville — mighty Casey has struck out.

The Baseball

Sandra Liatsos

I see it rise
to conquer space
like a rocket
in a race.

It hovers at
the peak of flight
almost past
my range of sight —

Then

down it dives
by air's command
to make a landing
in my hand.

from Teammates

Peter Golenbock

Stopping beside Jackie,
Pee Wee put his arm around
Jackie's shoulders.

An audible gasp rose up
from the crowd
when they saw
what Pee Wee had done.

Then there was silence.

Outlined on a sea of green grass
stood these two great athletes,
one black,
one white,
both wearing the same
team uniform.

"I am standing by him,"
Pee Wee Reese said to the world.
"This man is my teammate."

Great Pitches

J. Patrick Lewis

The fastball
          that you hope to poke
          is smoke

The curveball
          that you thought was there
          is air

The knuckler
          wobbling up to you
          can dipsy-do

The screwball
          an ironic twist
          hits your fist

The sinker
          comes as some surprise:
          it dies

The let-up pitch
          you can't resist?
          You missed

The spitball
          that by law's forbidden
          (is hidden)

Don Larsen's Perfect Game

Paul Goodman

Everybody went to bat three times
except their pitcher (twice) and his pinch hitter,
but nobody got anything at all.
Don Larsen in the eighth and ninth looked pale
and afterwards he did not want to talk.
This is a fellow who will have bad dreams.
His catcher Berra jumped for joy and hugged him
like a bear, legs and arms, and all the Yankees
crowded around him thick to make him be
not lonely, and in fact in fact in fact
nothing went wrong. But that was yesterday.

The Umpire

Milton Bracker

The umpire is a lonely man
Whose calls are known to every fan
Yet none will call him Dick or Dan
     In all the season's games.
They'll never call him Al or Ed
Or Bill or Phil or Frank or Fred
Or Jim or Tim or Tom or Ted —
     They'll simply call him names.

Two to Nothing

Lillian Morrison

Catcher, the ball caller
     knees bent, squatting;
Pitcher, a slider guider
     peering, plotting.
First up, a pop up
     hung his head, spit.
Next up, a bloop looper
     got a cheap hit.
Then came a bunt dumper
     out at first base
     (a runner with pep
     but out by a step).
Then came the power,
     the big number one
slammed a slow pitch
     for a towering home run.

Overdog

Tony Johnston

Overdog Johnson is a guy
who always wins
but hardly tries.

Pitcher sails it.
Johnson nails it.
Whack!
Homerun!

Pitcher steams it.
Johnson creams it.
Thwack!
Homerun!

Pitcher smokes it.
Johnson pokes it.
Smack!
Homerun!

Pitcher fires it.
Johnson wires it.
Crack!
Ho-hum.

The Base Stealer

Robert Francis

Poised between going on and back, pulled
Both ways taut like a tightrope-walker,
Fingertips pointing the opposites,
Now bouncing tiptoe like a dropped ball
Or a kid skipping rope, come on, come on,
Running a scattering of steps sidewise,
How he teeters, skitters, tingles, teases,
Taunts them, hovers like an ecstatic bird,
He's only flirting, crowd him, crowd him,
Delicate, delicate, delicate, delicate — now!

Mighty Joe

Lee Bennett Hopkins

Mighty Joe
DiMaggio
will not play
Old Timers Games.

He knows
time changed

> his aim
> his stance
> his swing —

he knows

> TIME

changes

> every-
> thing.

Instruction

Conrad Hilberry

The coach has taught her how to swing,
run bases, slide, how to throw
to second, flip off her mask for fouls.

Now, on her own, she studies
how to knock the dirt out of her cleats,
hitch up her pants, miss her shoulder
with a stream of spit, bump
her fist into her catcher's mitt,
and stare incredulously at the ump.

The Last Poem

Tom Meschery

When

        the game has ended
        and the roar of the crowd
        has faded into the past
        and only the cleaning brooms
        click-clack echoes
        on the empty rows of seats
        drumming through
        the dim-lit concrete corridors
        of the stadium what

then?

Permission Acknowledgments

Every effort has been made to trace the ownership of all copyrighted material and to secure the necessary permissions to reprint these selections. In the event of any question arising as to the use of any material, the editor and the publisher, while expressing regret for any inadvertent error, will be happy to make the necessary correction in future printings.

Grateful acknowledgment is made to the following for permission to reprint the material listed below:

SAMUEL ALLEN for "To Satch (Or American Gothic)." Used by permission of the author, who controls all rights.

ATHENEUM PUBLISHERS for an excerpt from "At Little League." Reprinted with permission of Atheneum Publishers, an imprint of Macmillan Publishing Company, from *Catch Me a Wind* by Patricia Hubbell. Copyright © 1968 by Patricia Hubbell.

CURTIS BROWN, LTD., for "Mighty Joe" by Lee Bennett Hopkins. Copyright © 1993 by Lee Bennett Hopkins. Used by permission of Curtis Brown, Ltd.

ISABEL JOSHLIN GLASER for "Playing Outfield" and "Prediction: School P. E." Used by permission of the author, who controls all rights.

SALLY GOODMAN for "Don Larsen's Perfect Game" from *Collected Poems* by Paul Goodman. Reprinted by permission of Sally Goodman.

HARCOURT BRACE JOVANOVICH, PUBLISHERS, for an excerpt from *Teammates* by Peter Golenbock, copyright © 1990 by Golenbock Communications, Inc., reprinted by permission of Harcourt Brace Jovanovich, Inc.

CONRAD HILBERRY for "Instruction." Used by permission of the author, who controls all rights.

TONY JOHNSTON for "Overdog." Used by permission of the author, who controls all rights.

J. PATRICK LEWIS for "Great Pitches." Used by permission of the author, who controls all rights.

LOTHROP, LEE AND SHEPARD BOOKS for "Let's Go, Mets" and "Two to Nothing" from *The Break Dance Kids* by Lillian Morrison. Copyright © 1985 by Lillian Morrison. By permission of Lothrop, Lee and Shepard Books, a division of William Morrow & Company, Inc.

TOM MESCHERY for "The Last Poem" from *Over the Rim*. Copyright © 1968 by Popular Library.

THE NEW YORK TIMES COMPANY for "The Umpire" by Milton Bracker. Copyright © 1962 by The New York Times Company. Reprinted by permission.

MARIAN REINER for "The Baseball" by Sandra Liatsos. Copyright © 1993 by Sandra Liatsos. Used by permission of Marian Reiner for the author.

THE LITERARY ESTATE OF MAY SWENSON for "Analysis of Baseball" by May Swenson. Copyright © 1971 by May Swenson. By permission of The Literary Estate of May Swenson.

WESLEYAN UNIVERSITY PRESS for "The Base Stealer" from *The Orb Weaver* by Robert Francis. Copyright © 1948 by Robert Francis. By permission of University Press of New England.